Claire –

THANKS FOR BEING MY SUNSHINE

A You Matter Letter Written By:

Annie

Wiggle Warrior® Books

An imprint of Look for the Good Project, Inc.

Text copyright © 2021 by Anne Kubitsky. Illustrations and photographs owned or licensed by Anne Kubitsky. All rights reserved. No part of this book may be reproduced, scanned or distributed in any printed or electronic form without permission in writing from the author.

lookforthegoodproject.org

Your Mission: Finish This Book!

This book is not complete. In the next two weeks, your mission is to finish it. Pick a person in your life who makes you feel safe and loved. This is your "Sunshine Person." Use this book to write them a You Matter Letter. Write in this book, color in it, tape some special photos to the pages... do whatever you need to do to make this book your own. When you are done, take some time to read this book to your sunshine person... and see what happens!

Use pencils and crayons to make this book your own!

Dear ___Claire___

You matter to me. I wrote you a letter and put it in this book so that you can keep it for a really long time.

I hope you enjoy it!

                                            Love,

                                            ___Annie___

When I put my hands on my heart and think about the people who matter to me...

You come to mind.

(Here's a picture of us)

7

It feels like there's an invisible string that connects your heart to mine.

8

I can feel it whenever I think of you.

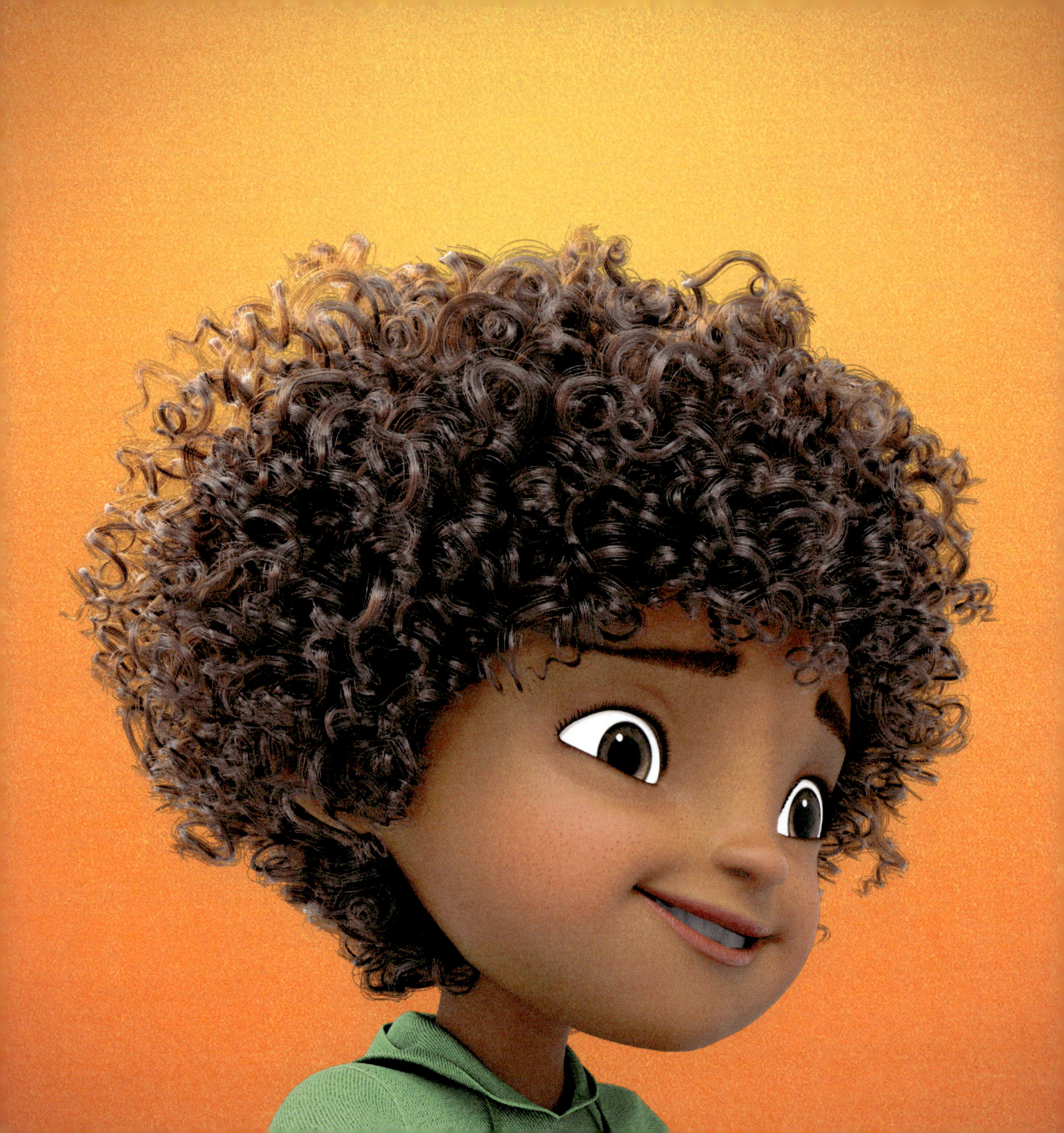

You matter to me because you make me feel seen and appreciated.

You make my life better when you do this:

> You are like the glue connecting your friends + family + I am so grateful for all your efforts to connect!

And this:

> Being so kind to me when I was going through my breakup + all the mess with my parents. Talking to you made me feel loved + cared for in a way that meant so much.

Whenever I'm feeling upset...

15

16

You'll sit with me
until I'm ready...

I'M FINE

to face my **STRESS**

I'M FINE

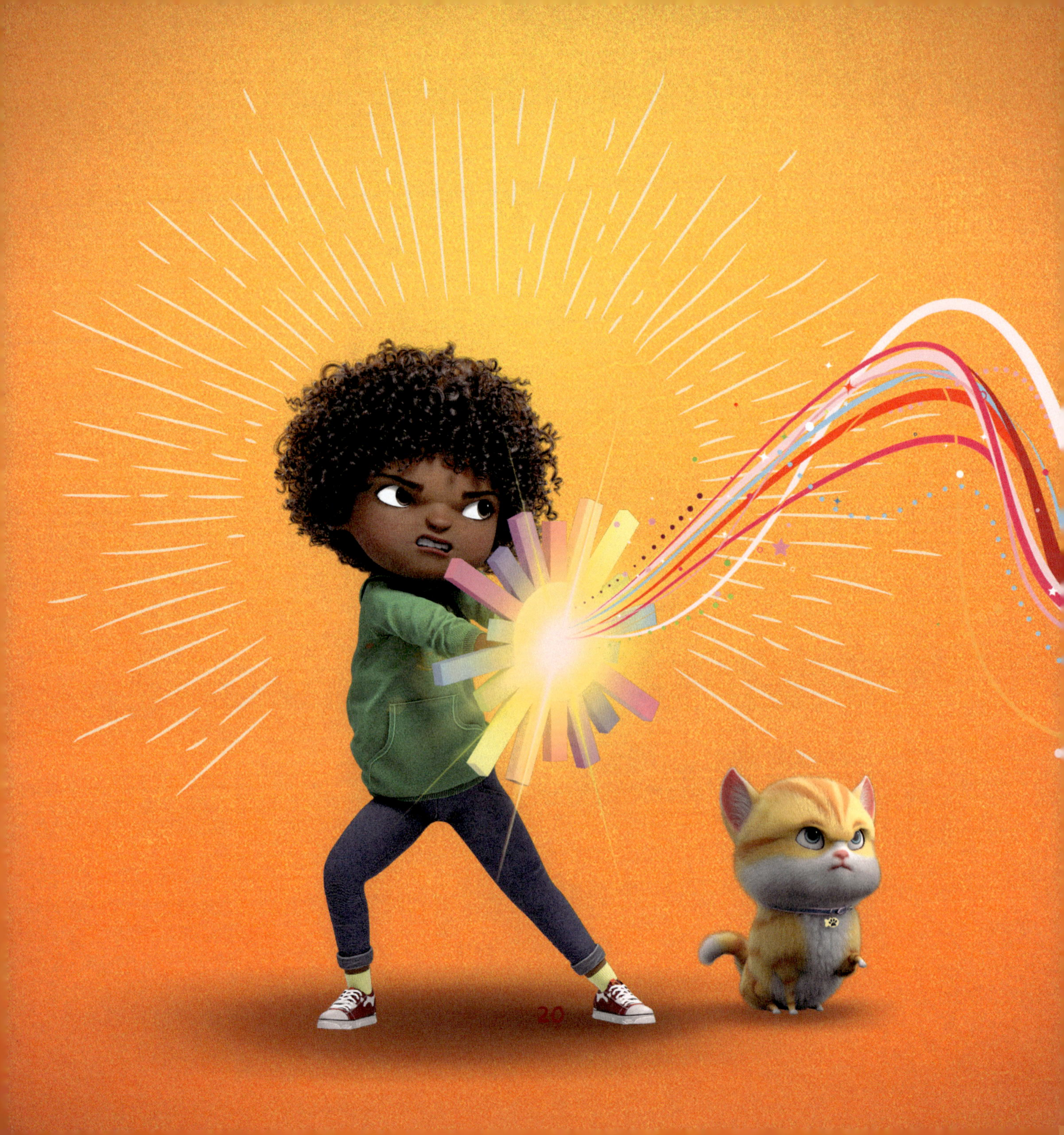

and wiggle it
into **STRENGTH.**

By supporting me while I learn how to make Sunshine Choices...

Feelings Wheel

MAD — I CHOOSE TO BE CLEAR & ASSERTIVE
Advocate for Myself When Something Isn't Fair
- Annoyed
- Frustrated
- Angry
- Enraged
- Apathetic

ICKY — I CHOOSE TO BE HONEST & SELF-PROTECTIVE
Protect Myself When Something Isn't Right
- Disgusted
- Resentful

GLAD — I CHOOSE TO BE GRATEFUL & GENEROUS
Connect With Others When I'm Feeling Safe
- Happy
- Grateful
- Inspired
- Giddy
- Excited

AFRAID — I CHOOSE TO BE BRAVE & CURIOUS
Find Courage to Learn & Grow
- Uncertain
- Anxious
- Afraid
- Panicked
- Overwhelmed

SAD — I CHOOSE TO BE RESILIENT & KIND
Care for Myself When It's Time to Let Go
- Heartbroken
- Rejected
- Lonely
- Sad
- Disappointed

...you're helping me
discover my own strength
(and sunshine!).

25

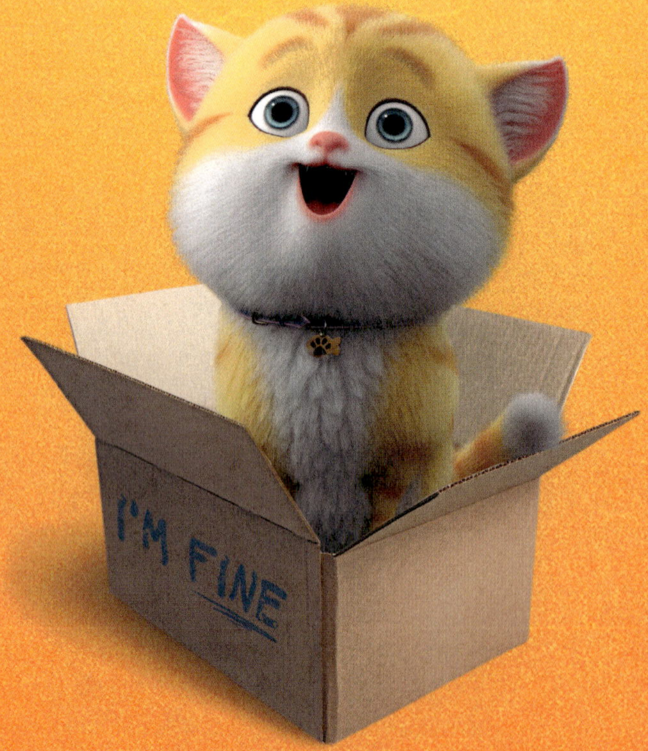
I'M FINE

Thanks for always
being there for me.

It's so nice to be back in touch!

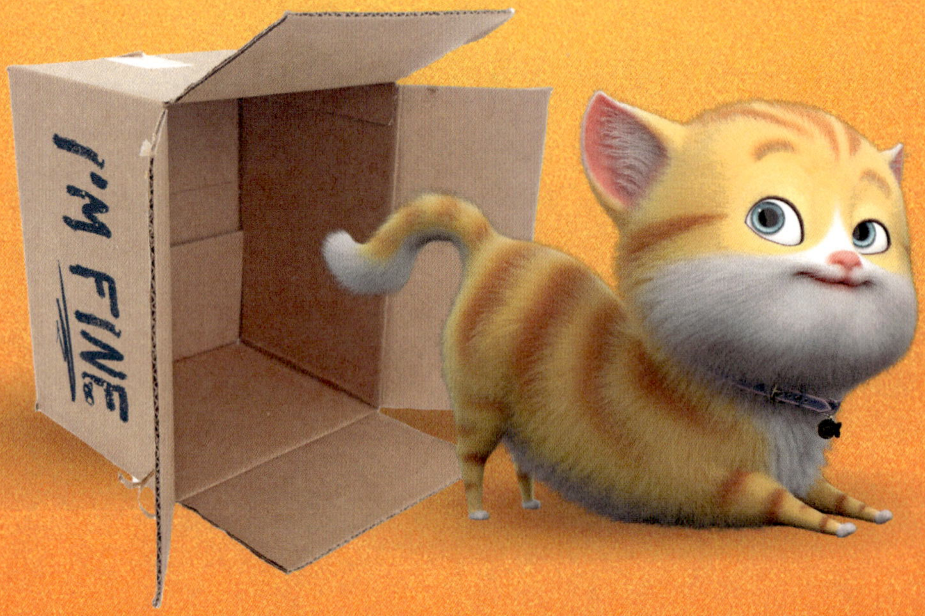
I'M FINE

And for giving me the confidence to learn and grow.

30

YOU MATTER!

*Love,
Annie*

You matter to me because...

You are my cousin + friend + I am so proud to know you. Thank you for sharing your big heart + big family with me. Sending you a big HUG!   ♡ Annie

If you're feeling exhausted, unproductive, or messier than usual, just remember - you have been supporting me through a global pandemic. You have been looking out for me <u>every</u>. <u>single</u>. <u>day</u>. And because of this, I trust you.

Thank you for caring for me and sharing your sunshine with me.

Who is YOUR Sunshine Person? Sunshine People Are:

- Consistently kind to you
- Consistently make you feel calm & safe
- Love you just as you are
- Respect your limits and boundaries
- Always looking out for your wellbeing
- Not afraid of stress & can be supportive when you're struggling
- Make you feel seen, understood & appreciated
- Never try to hurt you
- Not jealous of your joy and know how to celebrate your achievements
- Warm and nurturing (like sunshine!)
- Apologize for their mistakes and make amends
- Proactively work to earn your trust

35

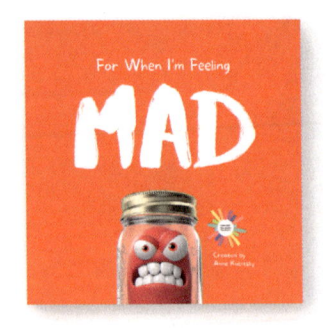

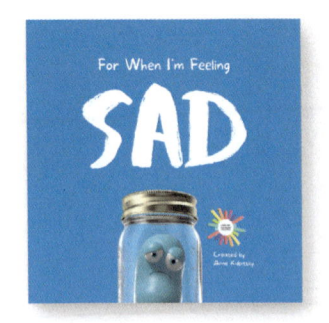

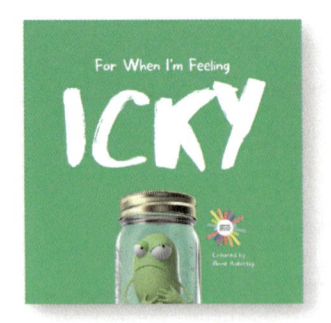

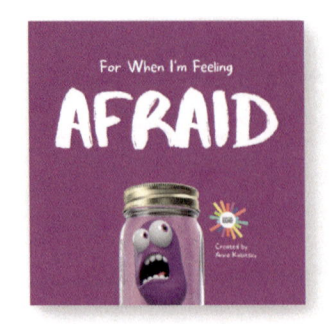

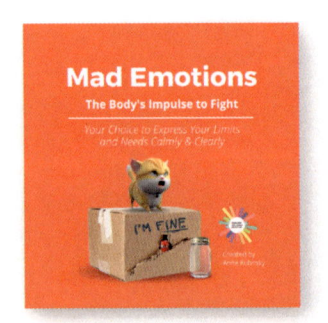

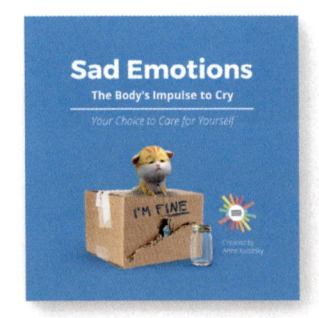

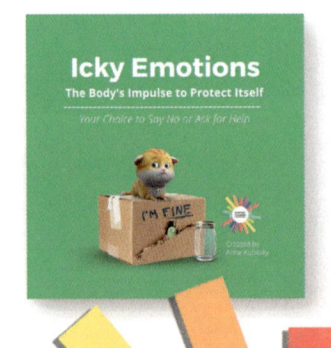

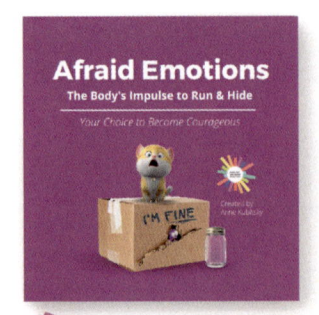

GREAT WORK!

To learn about our Wiggle Warrior® Program, or to access free content online, please visit our website.

LOOK FOR THE GOOD® PROJECT.ORG

ANNE KUBITSKY
Author & Creator

Anne is the Founder & CEO of Look for the Good Project, Inc. She has received numerous awards for her innovative efforts to create social change, including the "Point of Light Award" - a community service award originating out of The White House. She holds a BA in biology and philosophy from Smith College, with additional training in graphic design and illustration from Paier College of Art. Anne has been studying meditation, yoga, psychology, and a variety of therapeutic models for the last 21 years. Look for the Good Project is her effort to support the larger community with the tools she has discovered along the way. Anne is donating 100% the proceeds from this book to Look for the Good Project. Please visit lookforthegoodproject.org for more info.

ADDITIONAL CREDITS

Special thanks to ANMP, a group of talented artists in Europe. For over a year, Anne worked with ANMP (despite a 6 hour time difference!) to flesh out all of these characters and bring this book to life. The little girl and cat character were designed by artist, Song Na (bravo!).

Editing & Support: Kari Yacawych & Tess Morrison

STAY CLOSE TO THE

PEOPLE (AND ANIMALS)

WHO FEEL LIKE SUNSHINE!